FREEDOM FROM PORN ADDICTION

Joshua Snell

Snellster

CONTENTS

THE SCOPE AND PURPOSE OF THIS BOOK

I want to make the scope and purpose of this book clear from the beginning. So, let me begin by explaining what this book is not.

This book is not a quick fix. You will not become super spiritual and completely incapable of watching pornography again after reading this book. I do not hold *all* the answers; there are additional questions you may need to answer in your own life that are not mentioned in *Freedom from Porn Addiction*. This book is not the only one on the subject, and the author does not pretend to have a monopoly of knowledge on the issue. There is no one-size fits all approach to finding freedom from porn addiction because the root causes can be different for different people. But there are some common thoughts, actions, and cycles that keep people trapped regardless of the first thing that brought them into pornography.

What I am presenting you with is a tool. A tool requires something to act upon it in order for it to work. If you want to use a hammer, then *you* have to use the hammer. If you want to use this book to help deliver you from porn addiction, then *you* must use this book. You cannot passively overcome your porn addiction. You must take this tool and actively participate with it. It is not magic. It is difficult work. But it is work that will pay off in the end by liberating you from an addiction to pornography.

I also want to make it clear from the beginning that I am talking about watching porn. A person can stop watching porn and still struggle with other sexual issues and pressures in their life, such as masturbation or idolizing sex. Ending your addiction to porn is like destroying a huge pillar which helps to feed these other sexual lies in your life. But do not think that by stopping your addiction to porn you will instantly stop masturbating or making sex a dangerously consuming part of your life. It's a first and significant step in that direction, but the journey cannot be made in a single step. Have hope but do not be disillusioned.

I am a Christian. I do not hide that. While I use language in this book that is Christian, it is not a book written exclusively *for* Christians. The times when that language come up, it is where it is unavoidable. Any investigation into the human condition requires exploring deep principles of reality. At the very least, this book will offer a reader of any worldview a good ground to cultivate critical thinking about their own beliefs and practices.

Finally, this book is intended not only for the porn addicts themselves, but also for others—parents, spouses, and teachers. The worldview correction in this book is not only capable of healing the addict, but it is also an effective tool for preventing addiction in the lives of those not yet caught in pornography. In addition to that, I want to note that while I am writing this from the perspective of a man, the tools to freedom I offer in this book are in no way exclusive to men. I have both men and women in mind, as both are caught in porn addiction. By going through this process, both men and women will better understand their addiction. They will also be in a position to cultivate more empathy, which we will see is vital to overcoming porn addiction. This is a book for everyone. This book is about freedom.

Chapter 1 Homework:

On a piece of paper: Make a list of all the people who are affected by your porn addiction, the way they are affected, and how being free from your porn addiction might improve each relationship.

Answer the following question(s) for yourself:

1. Will you decide to follow all the steps in this book even if they are difficult and scary? Yes, or no?

OPENING THOUGHTS

When a child shows up to a circus, he's told to expect a good time: The lights are flashing, music is playing and a general air of excitement passes through the entire audience. Giant tent flaps are thrown open and an elephant comes out; it dances, parades, and is even fed fruit on the stage with other exotic animals. The child sees this and imagines to himself, "I wish I could join the circus. Those elephants are so cool; they have such an interesting life." In reality, however, that elephant the boy is watching in the circus tent will later be in a much different situation. He will be placed in a restrictive pen, beaten with canes by the circus ringleaders and starved in order to perform for food. If the child could throw the tent doors back and see the nature of the circus behind the scenes, he would see that this elephant was an animal that hated its job, came to despise circus workers, and wanted to leave.

Pornography is a lot like that circus. We see it sexed up with lights and music, and society tells us that we are supposed to expect excitement and a good time from it. It looks great and everyone is happy. But if we could see behind the scenes, we would realize that porn is not a happy circus. It's a place of pain and suffering for everyone involved. Men and women are forced to do things they never wanted to do. They are abused, drugged, and mistreated. We must do something to stop the abuse. The only way to end this is by going behind what the circus tent shows us and being honest with ourselves about the nature of pornography. Imagine the child sitting in the circus. Now imagine the child getting up and going behind the curtain to see the real nature of the circus. The boy sees the elephants being tortured and abused.

However, none of this bothers the boy at all. He goes back and continues watching the circus. That is what happens to many men and women in our culture. They see porn as a bad thing or hear reports about the damaging effects of porn—but it doesn't change them. Why?

There is a problem that faces us. It is the problem at the heart of overcoming pornography that must be dealt with before anything else can become effective. Our society has cultivated a lack of empathy between people. What that means is that we can look at pain and not care, because it is not our pain, or it's not pain that we can stop or pain that we can relate to. Many times, however, it is simply this—though we don't say it out loud: "It's not real pain because that's not a real person or a person I know, so I can disconnect from any responsibility for their trauma and keep watching the circus."

Empathy is our ability to identify with another person, to relate to their feelings and recognize that they think and feel, too. We can even develop empathy for things that don't exist, such as characters we can relate to in a well-written novel. Empathy is selfless and considers other people. Porn is inherently selfish. As a result of its selfish nature, the freedom to our addiction must come from looking outside of ourselves. We need to understand the humanity and value of others. If we are self-absorbed, then men and women in the porn industry will be objects for our pleasurable consumption. Without empathy, without an understanding that they feel pain and need love, we will fall into this trap. Empathy is necessary to overcome our addiction.

If you are a Christian, for example, you can be shown countless passages of the Bible where you need to treat others with respect, help the needy, and love unconditionally. But if you do not identify the person on the screen of your porn video as a real human being, who needs to be treated in these ways, then no Bible passages or teachings will change you. For example, I can truly believe that it is evil to abuse people. However, I won't even feel bad, let alone be moved to change, if I see a person with as much humanity as a rock—a non-human being. It's like when I kick a rock down the street. I don't care about the rock I am kicking. It doesn't bother me if it chips or gets smashed by an oncoming car or even if I lose it and never see it again. I'll just get another rock. It's an object. An unfeeling thing. Who cares?

I am fully aware that abuse is a terrible thing, but when I am kicking the rock I don't feel I'm abusing anyone; it's just a rock. In like manner, for many who watch pornography, the men and women on the screen have no more humanity to them than a rock. They are objects used for temporary pleasure, like a candy bar or a rock that bounces funny when you kick it. A person watching porn can understand every aspect of good moral conduct toward others who they know personally or interact with. They will treat those around them in socially acceptable ways. They do this because they understand these are people they live with, work with, see in their community, and, of course, they'll treat them like a human being should be treated. But the person in the porn video is not a human being to them. There are reasons for this disconnect. It's not random and, fortunately, it can be reversed. It may take a long time to reverse it. One reason for the loss of humanity in porn actors is a misconception of porn's nature.

As a single man, I was always confused because people would tell me that I needed to get rid of my sexual passions to avoid porn and other sin. But I knew that was wrong from simple observation. I knew married men trapped in porn addiction, and I remembered a time long ago, as a single young man, when porn didn't bother me. So porn was not then all about sex; there was more to it. The advice I had received from well-meaning people failed again and again, not because they were necessarily wrong, but because they did not treat the root of the issue. The root of the issue was in me, the addict.

Porn is a distortion of sex; it is taking a good thing and making it ugly. Porn is taking a real action and replacing it with only a faint perception of that real action. For example, when I look at an object under the water, it appears distorted from its original shape and size. It may be larger or smaller than it really is, and it may be disproportionate to its real shape. Imagine looking into the water and seeing an object that you've never seen before. You would probably not be able to tell the intended function of that object and its true purpose. Likewise, porn distorts sex in the minds of those who watch it. They see sex in this distorted view.

The answer to overcoming porn addiction is not getting rid of our sexual desires but rather getting those desires in line with God's desire for us. It is important to focus on correcting what has been made wrong.

A result of correcting the wrongness of porn is that we can save many who are broken. We might not be able to save all the broken people in the world from being hurt, but we can save some of them. It is a sin against God and a crime against humanity and our own virtue to use imperfection as an excuse to do nothing about the suffering in this world. Porn is a world of misery and we can stop. Pornography is a system built on the exploitation of childhood trauma, broken children, and manipulation. Pornography takes men and women who have sometimes been assaulted and traumatized and then either forces or coerces them into a perpetual cycle of pain and mental agony.

The porn industry is so huge that it can be a daunting task to try and fight. Where does one begin? It is financially larger than any other media outlet; it's socially untouchable by pop culture; and is physically protected by criminal organizations across the world.

Equally daunting is the fight within the man himself who says, "I want to break free from pornography." It is mentally taxing, emotionally draining, physically sickening to be trapped in the world or grasp of pornography and desperately desiring to get out. How do you stop when you know something is wrong, but you do it anyway?

The addict can always be healed. Freedom from porn addiction can happen no matter how prevalent eroticism is in society.

The world of freedom from pornography is blissful compared to fighting against addiction all the time. I was addicted to pornography as a young man, and it took me many years to break free. I tried advice I had received from peers, ministries, books – you name it, I tried. I felt helpless. No one had an answer for me. All my good intentions left me back exactly where I started. On my worst days I honestly felt in my heart that God Himself was incapable of helping. Somehow this was just how He made me and there was nothing I or He could do about it – that's hopelessness. But I found that the answer to my freedom was much greater than I ever imagined. I was not only liberated from the desire to watch porn but I was given a new understanding of my own identity and the world around me. I truly live now and was made into a new person. You can be too. When, in this book, you hear me speaking harshly, remember that I never, as Shakespeare said, jest at scars that never felt a wound. I have felt every wound I mention, and I have borne the weight of every step and requirement in this book upon my own shoulders first. I have found freedom. That is why I am different and have done what I once considered impossible. That is why you need to read, listen, and follow everything written here if you want to stop fighting and be free.

What is the difference between fighting and being free?

In the Bible, Jesus tells a parable about a man who goes on a journey and gives his servants money. Two of his servants take what they were given and get even more than what they have. Their master returns and is very happy with them. But the third servant takes his money, and because he is afraid, he digs a hole and hides the money inside. When his master returns, the master sees that the servant didn't do anything with what he had been given and the master becomes angry.

Similar to the servants, when we are free from unhealthy fear, we can be courageous to fight against evil without fear of exposure from secrets or falling back into the same cycle of failure we used to exist in. We can take our time and energy and invest in the fight against evil and corruption in this world and honestly become better people, loving those around us in renewed and closer ways each day. Fighting porn is like the third servant, we are hiding from situations that might make us fail again or expose the struggle we are dealing with. We are figuratively being chased around by fear all day. We are digging a hole and burying – or hiding – our lives inside, not free to live but only existing in a fight that seems to have no end. Being free from porn addiction will lead to our betterment and make our world a healthier place. Fighting against pornography addiction in your life will always lead to fear and failure and will continue in an exhausting cycle of defeats. This can be testified by millions of people trying the same things over and over while failing and fearing each day.

Don't settle for the ease of ignoring this book and the way out of your pornography addiction. Instead, strive for excellence and virtue in your life so that you can honestly say you excel in what it is to be a good man or woman and have no need to hide in shame. It is time to be free. I will show you how.

Chapter 2 Homework:

On a piece of paper, do the following exercises and answer the following questions:

1. List the ways you have been selfish by using pornography.
2. Write a short apology to everyone you have affected by using pornography and use the ways you've been selfish as examples in your apology. Confess your words here on paper.

Answer the following questions for yourself:

1. If you were not mentally and emotionally tied up in fighting porn addiction or watching porn, what is at least one thing you could do with that new mental and

emotional energy?

2. What dreams and talents could you pursue or perfect if you remove porn from your life?

WHAT'S IT ALL ABOUT?

There are three sections of thought that we must go through to overcome pornography addiction. Within these three sections are smaller ones. However, the outline of this book will be in three sections; one for each of the three major components we will address.

First, we must take responsibility for our actions. We have to admit that we are guilty of doing something wrong. We are the ones at fault for our actions. We can't blame it on other people.

Second, we need to have legitimate disgust for what we have done and for what porn is. We need to understand that our actions are evil and need to not happen again. This is not the same as feeling sorry for being caught, and it is not the same as feeling guilty. If you are caught and feel bad, then the emotion centers on you. And if you feel guilty and feel bad because of that, then again, the emotion centers around you. But you have to feel bad about the act itself, so that even if you were not caught doing it and even if you never did it again, the very existence of it would still be seen for the evil that it is. Only when you realize the evil in the thing itself can you see the fullness of the evil in your participation within that system.

Third, we need to see change in our actions. As obvious as this is to state, we must change our actions – that is, after all, the point of this book.

In this book I am going to explain the thought process that you will need to go through to initiate the change in your life and then a step – by – step list of actions that I took. Finally, I will finish with some closing thoughts of what you might experience and what you will need to know during the next weeks or months of your journey. Married or single, you can and you will be free. When you are, then you will understand yourself and your situation in a new light.

But first, let's address two words and three lines that we must discuss before healing can take place.

There is no homework for this chapter.

TWO DEPLORABLE WORDS

There is a world of difference between having a rational judgment that porn is bad and you should stop watching it and understanding how and why it is evil. We may acquire a judgment that porn is evil by hearsay, our parents, or church. These weak impressions of judgment are meaningless to help us in time of the temptation. They exist only in our heads, like an opinion. When opinion and desire compete for dominance in our minds, opinion will always lose. We must have an understanding or a sense of its evil in our hearts that moves us to repulsion and disgust of the sin and then a desire to change. This sense of evil is found by coming to terms with the reality of how hurtful the porn industry is to God, those abused in the industry, those dear to us, and ourselves. It is not enough to be repulsed at the idea of our guilt or being found out, but we must be repulsed and disgusted by the thing itself. If we are so disgusted by the evil in pornography that we no longer find it attractive, then we will not be tempted to watch pornography again. Opinions alone cannot give us such feelings, neither will excusing porn.

To come to grips with how evil porn is, we are required to stop addressing it as a non-existent problem or a problem where the responsibility to change is outside of ourselves. We cannot refer to it by anything other than what it is. Porn addicts commonly use vague words when describing their actions; this must stop because it hinders them from confronting evil in their life. I'm going to use two specific words I used and I hear many people use to cover up the specific evil of porn. There may be other words that use. If there are other words you need to stop using those words as well.

Here are two words that should not be used by anyone when talking about their addiction to pornography, and why:

1. Lust: This one is particularly popular for Christians, but is used by people of all backgrounds. What makes it harmful is that it is vague by definition, especially for English speakers. We use this word when we really have in mind a specific act of evil we have committed. It hides what we've really done.

Using the word lust is vague and so it hides the intensity of our porn addiction. It makes us feel good because everyone does bad things and so we are more comfortable saying we did something bad when we are not comfortable with the particular bad thing we did. It is a way to admit we did something wrong without having to be uncomfortable. But that is harmful. It makes us less responsible in our own eyes, and as a result, we don't feel as much of a need to change our actions. For example, in modern English a person can say I lusted after a cheeseburger or anything else that they wanted. Lust is a very weak word.

Did you watch porn? Then say so. Don't use these vague words to hide the truth. Saying the name of your sin and speaking openly about it, will make you become freer. Most of the shame that is associated with these problems is in that catastrophic thinking that if someone found out, they would reject me; therefore, we don't even really admit it to peers. That catastrophic thinking is only removed by facing the truth and speaking honestly and realizing that the sun will still rise tomorrow, and we will still be alive.

2. Tempted: When talking to peers many people will say they were tempted the week they met with their support group. Were you just tempted or did you give in to that temptation? You can't use the word "temptation" to describe the act of watching pornography and masturbating. That's giving in to temptation. It's like stealing a sports car and crashing after a night of

drug induced debauchery and then telling your friend the next morning, "Yeah man, I'll admit I was tempted to get a little crazy last night." Only say tempted if you were tempted but didn't give in. Otherwise, you are only telling the half-truth with the intention of deceiving. You're lying and it just keeps you in shame and further from freedom.

Chapter 4 Homework:

Answer the following question(s) for yourself:

1. When the author says, in the first paragraph of this chapter, "Opinions alone cannot give us such feelings, neither will excusing porn," what opinions or excuses have you entertained in the past? What are ways to strengthen your resolve today beyond mere opinion?
2. Write out on a piece of paper a confession of what you have actually done by watching porn and masturbating, make sure you do not say, "lust" or "tempted" but be clear and precise in what you've done. Then make an apology for these specific things.

THREE LIES

Now these are three lies we tell ourselves. In order for healing to be complete in our minds, we must address and correct these three lies.

1. "It's hopeless. I will never get free. It's just series of small victories and starting over again after I lose."

I want you to do an experiment with me. Imagine all the years of your life ahead of you. It is overwhelming to see all those years ahead for a young man and envisioning fighting addiction over that whole course of a lifetime. We live in a society that is saturated with sex in all aspects of life. Even ads for tenderloin cheeseburgers are designed to get your loins anything but tender. If the plan for staying free from pornography is that it will be done by escaping the influence of eroticism, then guess what, it is hopeless. It's simply the truth–escaping the influences of a sexed-up society is a hopeless cause, and you will never be free from that stimulus. It will, for the rest of your life, be a cycle of fighting with all your strength for a few days, a few weeks, maybe even of few months, and then you will still fall back into the cycle. You will receive an email or feel depressed or see something that is sexy enough on TV to get your gears turning, and then go fall in the cycle all over again.

So, why is "it is hopeless" a lie?

The statement "it's hopeless" is a lie because hiding from stimulus is not how to be free from pornography. If you want to fight against the world's influence, you will never win. The way to freedom is to kill your enemy, which means killing your desire for porn, not your desire for sex but your desire for that distortion of sex. When you are free from the desire to watch porn, then you are free to live the rest of your life from that day till death without having to worry about when you will encounter the next pornographic material and how you will deal with it. You don't have to fight an enemy that's dead. You only have to fight an enemy that is still alive.

2. "I need to hide what I am doing."

This is one of the easiest lies to believe. People who watch porn are filled with shame. We feel like garbage and believe that everyone else will shun us like a disease if they only knew what we did. The fact is, there are some people who would do this, but that is not everyone. It's better, anyway, to have people around you who care for you and the person you are becoming and not only the person you are or have been. A porn addict who is earnestly changing out of their addiction will for the rest of their life have that in their past; they cannot worry about it, they can only change into something new. I speak from experience. We will only be rejected by those who are shallow. In our honesty and openness we have freedom. Part of that freedom is the liberation from shame and anxiety. We are loved and accepted for who we really are. By admitting it, we know that we have stood with honesty and are accepted or rejected for who we really are.

Freedom from porn can not happen without exposing that it is happening. It is a problem that happens in secret and freedom can not happen in secret as well. This is a mistake many people make by trying to fix their porn addiction in private and even when they are doing good for a time, they are afraid of their computer or phone or when they will be tempted or afraid that someone will find out about their past. That is not freedom. By being open about what you did or what you are doing, you are free to pursue freedom and the weight that is off your chest is unbelievable.

3. "It doesn't hurt anyone."

This is actually the easiest lie for someone to rationalize. I had rationalized it. This is why.

I heard about the evils of porn from a lot of well-meaning people. But rarely, and not until the end, did it have any bearing on my concern. This was because I had been told something about porn that was untrue to my situation, and it allowed me a way out. I was told, and I hear this for many people, that if you start watching porn then down the road you will get into more and more deplorable things like bestiality, extremely violent sex acts, and homosexuality, just to name a few things that people said porn was a gateway for and I was destined to go into that gateway. It is true that this can happen to some people. Having worked in the mental health field and having been exposed to domestic violence and abuse, I know all too well what kinds of atrocities can be opened up and fueled by pornography. However, the sensationalist claims I heard made me think that I was okay. I didn't feel sensational in my addiction.

I only watched what I considered safe, heterosexual, non-violent porn. It was okay. I justified it to myself. The porn I watched was never included in anything "weird." As a result, when people listed off the sensationalist evils of pornography and effects I was destined for, I justified my actions with facts. I watched porn and had for a while, but never once watched and could never conceive of watching the stuff these people claimed I must now be wanting to watch. I didn't see my porn as the stuff they were talking about. Though I knew it was wrong, in my heart, it was too easy to justify. But I was wrong. It is all harmful, no matter what they show you on the screen.

I realized how I had just justified porn, too, and that scared me. I had sanctified porn in my heart. The word sanctify means to set something apart to approve of it. What I did, without realizing it, was I had sanctified an entire genre of pornography as good porn. I never use that term, but that's what it was in my mind. It was set apart from the rest of the bad porn that I wouldn't watch because my good porn was just regular heterosexual stuff that no one got hurt, and with that, I unknowingly approved of it.

The fact is, porn was not a gateway to these abominations for me. Another fact that I overlooked was that porn was an abomination in itself. The truth was, it is still evil and it is hurting a lot of people. Here are several ways that all porn hurts people – no matter what kind it is.

It hurts the heart of God. God does not take porn lightly. It grieves God every time somebody idolizes His creation and demonizes His children. Porn does both things. You participate in that when you watch porn.

Porn hurts you. You are changing the way you view the other sex. Porn changes the way men and women view each other and it's not good. Porn does not only affect you when you're watching it, but it affects the way you view the other sex in your life and in your community who might not be aware even watching porn. For men, it makes you compare other women to the women who you see in porn. It hinders positive relationships with women because you are not interested in a deep relationship, even if you want to, because you're always thinking about porn and sex; it will hurt your social interactions. It will hurt your self-esteem and self-respect. Every man who is into porn or has been into porn knows how much it affects your sense of self-worth and that affects peer relationships with women and other men.

It hurts your spouse or future spouse. If you do not change and stop watching porn, you will hurt your spouse. You are already hurting your spouse. This is particularly important for young men who are not yet married. You need to change now before you are married. If not, then you will do the same thing you do with other women, but to your spouse – comparing her to the women you see in pornography or your husband if you're a woman. This will hurt your relationship in every way including the way you view your spouse and your expectations in your marriage. Additionally, imagine getting caught by your spouse and the pain you will cause them and the shame you will bring on yourself.

Or imagine having to admit that you're addicted to pornography while in your relationship. It's too late for many to say they never watch porn, but imagine how much better it would be to honestly look at your spouse in the eye and say, that was part of my past, and not be lying. There is a huge difference.

It hurts society. By watching porn, you are helping to perpetuate a worldview with a lack of worth and an increase of violence against women and men in your society. You can't escape your support even by watching free porn. Even free porn is supplied by sponsors, and every time you visit a free website, you are letting the sponsors know it is good business to continuing to sponsoring porn to the masses. Women in porn are routinely physically hurt and ashamed; and the perspective of women in society is skewed into becoming objects used for gratification rather than being seen for who they are. Women are people made in the image of God with feelings, a past, a future, and dreams. Think about the way that porn affects you personally, and then think about how many men and women it affects in your society. It hurts the women in the videos themselves. Porn is physically breaking them down mentally, shaming them, and destroying their identity as women, replacing it as the identity of a mere object. Who is there in your own life that you love? Do you have a mother, grandmother, or daughter that you would try to protect from abuse? These are real women just like your family. They feel pain; they have dreams other than what they're doing. There was a day when they were little children who wanted to grow up to be a doctor or a mother or someone, anyone, who is not an abused object for others pleasure and consumption. These women do not deserve to be abused – no one does.

Chapter 5 Homework:

Answer the following questions for yourself:

1. How can you keep a healthy desire for sex while

destroying your unhealthy desire for porn? What are your desires in porn and identify the evils of the distortion of sex within porn.

2. If you have not confessed to someone about your porn addiction, then do that. Find someone who is trustworthy like a close friend or a pastor. Be released from the chains of fear and live in the freedom of the light.

3. Identify the ways that porn is hurting you and specific steps you can take to find healing from that hurt. The answer to this question will be very personal to each person's journey.

PART ONE: ADMIT IT

Healing cannot happen without admitting that we are the problem. We are looking to fix what is wrong. This truth is evident in all aspects of life. Problems are what need fixing, not non-problems. We try to find problems and fix them when something is not working the way we want it to. If we have a broken arm and we blame our pain on our big toe, then we are setting ourselves up for failure because we can try to fix, wash, and cast our toe as much as we want while the arm only gets worse. We will have a beautiful, shiny toe at the end of the day, but we will still have a crippled and ugly arm from not treating our injury. Blame must be given where it's due in order for healing to start. If we blame our porn addiction on something or someone else, then we will not fix the real problem. The real problem is us. We are selfish. We are willing to get pleasure at the expense of others and use them as objects, not treating them as the human beings they are. As viewers of porn, we are at fault. Don't let this make you feel bad, but let it stir you to action. You do not watch porn because "you're a man" or "you're a woman" or because you're hopelessly addicted. You watch porn because you desire porn more than anything else. Pornography is the antithesis or exact opposite of manhood and womanhood. And no one is hopelessly addicted to it. I want to focus on the lie of hopeless addiction. Let's address the issue of "Why can't I stop watching porn?" I like this question because it's one that I asked myself, and after talking to other men, I feel everyone asks it. Finding the answer rocked my worldview. I had to be humble enough to realize I didn't understand the way my mind worked. I hope you can be open to carefully reading and learning in this chapter, too, because it will change your life, and if you're not open to being teachable, then you will not learn anything.

My confusion and inability to answer that question came from poor theology and philosophy. That sounds snooty, but it's just the proper way of saying that I really needed to understand myself and the world better. None of my mentors had ever taught me about this—because they themselves either didn't know or were unable to articulate it properly. The answer came, believe it or not, after meditating on several readings from the Bible and the classics. If I've scared you with that statement, trust me and please keep reading. We desire to watch pornography. We desire to not watch pornography. Our desires are competing for dominance in our minds. As humans, we will always choose our strongest and most immediate desire. For example, if you are in an alleyway and a man pulls a gun on you asking for money, then you will most likely give it to him. This isn't because you don't have a desire for your money, but the desire to save your life is stronger than your desire for your money. It is a much more immediate desire as well. The money is just money, and it can be replaced later. However, if a child with a water gun demanded your money, then you would probably not surrender your money because your desire for your money is not in competition with your desire for survival. In the Bible, Paul discusses his own similar struggle in his letter to the church in Rome, "For that which I do I know not: for not what I would, that do I practice; but what I hate, that I do" (Romans 7:15 ASV). Our lives are full of moments when we have conflicting desires. If Paul's frustration was dealing with porn, we could paraphrase him saying to himself, "You idiot, why did you do that again? You didn't want to do that, so why did you? Man, c'mon, Paul, why do you keep doing what you know you're going to hate yourself for?" The reason for the frustration with many men today regarding pornography is that there are several desires competing for action at once. To overcome porn, we must understand that it is a fight of desires. It's not an on and off switch where one desire is absent and the other is present. We feel the struggle to not watch porn. We are aware of the battle of desires.

The desire for not watching porn can even be stronger ninety-nine percent of the time. But in the moments of vulnerability, it becomes weaker and the desire for watching porn becomes the strongest and, without a doubt, the most immediate. At that moment, we succumb; we watch porn. We are at fault because we desire to watch porn more than the desire to not watch porn. It is a fault because it is a distortion of what manhood and womanhood are. But just like any distortion in our character, it can be corrected. In the next section we will look at why our desire to watch porn is a fault of ours and why it is so powerful in our lives. We will also see how to escape the prison of pornography.

Chapter 6 Homework:

You need to make your desires against porn be more intense and more immediate than desiring porn.

Answer the following questions for yourself:

1. What are the desires that draw you away from porn? How can you increase the intensity of those desires?
2. What are the places in your life where you are most vulnerable to desiring to watch porn and masturbate? Is it the shower, the bedroom, even the commute? Whatever it is, identify practical ways to *immediately* remove yourself from those situations.

PART TWO: SORROW AND HOPE

The desire to watch pornography will always win. It is such a powerful desire and feels so immediate that we will always give in each time the battle begins tipping, even the slightest, in that direction. Does that mean we are hopeless? If we are trying to fight against the desire of pornography, then, yes, it is hopeless. But if we no longer desired to watch pornography, then we would not have this battle ever again. We will have freedom for the rest of our lives. Sun Tzu, the great Chinese strategist, once said, "If your opponent is more powerful than you, avoid a confrontation." In my life I wanted to stop watching porn, but I didn't do anything about my desire to watch porn. I read the Bible, and I knew in my heart that it was wrong. But I really didn't feel bad about it until after the fact, and then it was a burden. In the moment of decision, however, when the desires were battling, that brokenness from the last time didn't seem real and didn't seem to matter. In overcoming porn, it is essential that we dismantle it as that strong and immediate desire. This is an obvious statement, but true. You will never watch porn if you are not attracted to porn. Duh, you might be saying now. But keep reading. If porn is evil, then why are we attracted to it? Some will say that it is because it is evil that we are attracted to it. It is a rush. Well, that's true, but not entirely so. Very few people who watch porn are also addicted to murder, even though that may be a huge rush to some. Nor would they shoot up their arms with heroine, though this, too, is evil and addicting. What is the difference, then, between those two issues and porn? Why a desire for the one and not for the others? The answer is in our understanding of what porn is and the consequences of it. I don't mean the statistics of pornography. I mean the real toll it takes women and men, and the reality of who they target for their performers. The second step to overcoming your porn addiction is in legitimate sorrow for what you have done. This is not self-condemnation, but it is an understanding of how messed up this world really is and how messed up the thing is that you have been doing. If you get nothing else out of this section, just come away with this one thing—empathy. Empathy is the ability to understand and relate to the feelings of another. I learned the truth about the pain women in the porn industry go through. The trauma many of them experience in their childhoods, and the pain that all of them experience once they are inside the industry. That knowledge changed me. I found humanity in the women who were having sex on the screen. The women were no longer things for my addiction; they were hurting people being forced or coerced into a life of shame and perpetual pain. From that moment forward, my addiction was only a few months away from being completely washed away.

Two things happened to me that changed my life forever by revealing the truth. I was exposed to the reality of how the porn industry many times takes people who are vulnerable, and sometimes even homeless or runaways, and exploits them. After being exposed to this reality, I was driving to work one morning and looked out the window at the freeway exit. There, standing on the corner, was a woman holding a sign. It looked as if she hadn't showered in days. She stared at her feet, and the sign in her hands read something like, "Need food, anything will help." I realized this woman was the same kind of woman who was in much of porn: hurting, desperate, in need of help and protection. A deductive argument fired its way to the forefront of my brain. It was simple logic.

If this woman offered to give you oral sex in exchange for food and shelter, you would say no and give her food and shelter and protect her from men who would take advantage of her.

The women in the porn videos are selling themselves like that.

Conclusion: What am I doing?

The gravity of my thoughts pulled to that idea all morning. I had figuratively been preying on homeless and desperate women when I watched porn. I went to shelters and fed the homeless with my church, yet of these, were the very ones that I was watching on my computer–the tired, the poor, those yearning to breathe free. Those on the computer merely wore the mask of makeup and hygiene. That revelation startled me. My sin was far more evil than I had ever believed it to be. That meant one terrible thing I didn't want to confess. I was far more evil than I had ever believed myself to be.

I started only then to see the women as human beings with souls, broken childhoods, people who were helpless and should have been cared for but, instead, were being taken advantage of. How would I feel about taking advantage of the girl whose father beat her? A girl who had been victimized over and over again by either family, friends, or strangers? Was that attractive? Did I think it was hot to exploit a girl who was a runaway because she couldn't cope with molestation or a broken family or was forced to sell her body to feed her children? That was called is prostitution and, in truth, that's what porn is.

The mask fell off. The women were no longer objects. They were real women with sometimes tortuous pasts and vulnerable pain on those videos who, as a man, I should be helping and not exploiting. I was being a predator without even knowing it. With my ignorance lifted, I could not go back. Not only did I see the consequences of my actions and the reality of what I had been doing, but I was truly disgusted by it. I could not go back to my old ways.

I could excuse any statistic because they were just numbers to me. I didn't really associate the numbers with real people. But when faced with the reality that these women are wounded, hurting, and need to be cared for, that they once were children playing with toys and had dreams of being something other than abused, then my soul could not ignore the virtue within it. We have a natural desire to protect those who are defenseless and to be vehemently disgusted at the exploitation of the hurting. All that is needed to defeat the desire to watch porn is realizing what porn really is: Participation in the abuse and exploitation of another human being.

Chapter 7 Homework:

Answer the following questions for yourself:

1. Who is the most vulnerable and innocent person you know? Answer yes or no whether you would abuse that person so they are able to survive.
2. Don't look at porn again as the circus, instead, realize that these are people who were once vulnerable and innocent. Write on a piece of paper that you will not take advantage of them.

PART THREE: THE CHANGE

As you start this section, I want you to take a minute and reflect. Don't condemn yourself for anything you've done in the past. Simply think for a moment about the reality that these are real people, many with tormented pasts and very painful childhoods, who have had that pain exploited. Just imagine them as a child crying in their bed at night, wishing they could escape their situation and to someday have a wonderful life. Stop and think about that for at least one minute, and then come back to the book.

Porn is disgusting. It preys upon the weak and the hurting and then exploits them for a profit. Repentance means turning away from what you have done in the past and not doing that evil thing anymore. In this section we are going to break down the process into seven steps and, if followed, they will kill your desire for pornography. Write all these down in a journal. These are not the end all; there may be things in your situation you also need to do, but these are seven things you need at very least.

Please take a piece of paper and or pencil and do these exercises after finishing the chapter.

1. Admit that you are responsible for your own actions and that you are responsible for watching pornography.
2. Ask yourself, "What do I desire most?" and write that question on the top of a piece of paper. Make two columns on that piece of paper. Write down "watching pornography" in one column and then in the other;

write down other great desires in your life. For example, having a healthy family, becoming a better man or woman, succeeding in life. Whatever desires compete with watching pornography, make sure to write down in that other column. Now pursue the things in that other column in your life with excellence. Make a plan on how you will accomplish those desires and put that plan into action. Do something.

3. Educate yourself on the truth about the porn industry and what both men and women go through. Don't forget the brokenness of these people's childhoods and the helplessness that comes in being trapped in a world of failure and suffering. Remember that each man and woman deserves the love of Jesus to be shown to them and our protection.

4. Think about those in your own life and community who are weak and vulnerable. Would you exploit them for sex if they come to you for protection or help? Would you feed a starving person only after they'd given up their body to you? Answer on a piece of paper, yes or no. If you don't know anyone personally who is in need, then get involved in your community and start helping people. You will find that having better connections with real people will help kill the fantasy of porn. When learning how to be a servant to others, you will be less attracted to porn, as porn is inherently selfish. If you said no, then realize that each time you're tempted to watch porn you are being put into a situation where you are living out that choice. What will you do?

If you answered yes to this question, then you really need to think about where you are in your heart. We all start somewhere on the path to freedom, some deeper in darkness than others. Some journeys are just longer than others. Changing you from desiring to exploit the innocent to freedom from that is an issue, however, is beyond the scope of this book. Seek clinical and biblical help.

5. Pray for the men and women who are being abused. Pray for their salvation, healing of their bodies, restoration of their broken hearts, rest from the pain and shame of their abuse, and encouragement to leave their situation. Even pray for those who are hurting them, that they, too, will change their hearts and stop. Here's a little something about the nature of evil. Evil will not stop by only taking innocent people out of their situations. Along with other actions, removing victims from these situations can help stop the cycle of abuse from continuing and they need to be removed from these situations. But removing a victim today will not stop an abuser from taking a new victim tomorrow. There is nothing that will stop people from becoming new victims of these abusers until the abusers stop abusing them. So pray for the abusers, too, because unless they are saved and changed, then there will always be this evil. Do this each day, but always do this when you feel tempted to watch porn again. Start praying for others and not for yourself. Remember porn is inherently selfish. I'm not saying it is selfish to pray for yourself, but I am saying reaching out and praying for others makes it much more difficult to watch porn when we're praying for the hurting person who would have been on that screen. It kills your selfish nature and bring to recall the evils of the act.

6. Get away from your computer when you feel even a hint of the desire to watch pornography. Put your computer where it can be seen by others. Go into public places and your neighborhoods; engage in the world around you. We live in a real world with real adventure. Go to a coffee shop and do homework rather than in your room; go to the gym rather than watch TV; go on a road trip with a friend and make a friend if you don't have any. Do

not just stay inside your home all weekend. And if need be, take a walk under the stars. Take cold showers for a while instead of hot ones if you feel the need. Before taking your phone to your room, turn off your Wi-Fi. Or get an old-fashioned alarm clock and don't keep your phone with you in your bedroom. Wherever the places are that you are most vulnerable to temptation make a place to remove yourself from those places and mitigate the risk by making it more difficult to watch porn in those places.

Feed your brain with good examples of men and women who are strong. Read the Bible and other good books about how to be honorable.

7. Remember that the choice you have to make, right from wrong, is a single decision each time. When you are tempted to watch porn it's easy to rationalize to yourself, "You have been good for a few days now," and then you let yourself watch porn. You have to remember that the choice to watch porn or not watch porn is a decision at that moment. Each choice to do the right thing or the wrong thing is your choice. These choices do not add up on scorecards. You have a new choice for each temptation. So make the right choice in each temptation.

Do not think about all your victories or all your failures. The desire for porn is quick, nearly impulsive. You have to be just as impulsive at saying no to your temptation if you want to avoid watching porn. If you hesitate for even a moment then you will fall into that temptation and watch porn. You have to be decisive and immediately leave the situation you're in. That's why number six on this list is so important; you have to have places away from technology, in the early days especially, to go when you are feeling the urge. Don't stop to rationalize or it will be too late.

Write on the piece of paper: When I am tempted to watch porn

I will leave.

Now you have already decided before the question even comes up so don't linger. Be as impulsive in your removing and detaching from the situation as the temptation is impulsive and you will avoid temptation. Do not deliberate, just act.

Chapter 8 Homework:

Put the seven steps into practice today.

THE IMPORTANCE OF PORN AND SALVATION

This chapter concerns everyone. Christians will certainly find it engaging, and non-Christians may find it engaging as well, or at the very least, they will find it entertaining. I am talking about the importance of keeping porn in its proper perspective with regards to salvation. There is a tendency to try and make one sin the tell-all about whether we are saved or not. In our American culture, porn has subtly come into this category. The idea is that you can't be watching porn and be saved at the same time. But this is a lie.

I have personally witnessed God move through men and women in their lives, and yet they still struggled to break free from pornography. God was present in their lives and they were certainly changed from the people they used to be. But still the issue of porn was a fight that had yet to be won. Did that mean that God was alive in them and the Holy Spirit had made these people new creations and yet they were not new creations? Of course not; that would be a contradiction. These men and women, who struggled with porn, were doing what other Christians do after trusting in Christ–they were becoming more like Christ. They were not perfect and neither is any man or woman whether they are addicted to porn or not. Sinful, too, is the glutton who is finding dopamine hits through countless donuts and quarts of ice cream. No one sin can be singled out as the tell-all about our relationship with Jesus. We all struggle and we all move closer to the cross in an uphill climb against the sin that remains. God-fearing men and women can struggle with porn. I went on missions trips, led Bible studies, and had a great prayer life, all while on the losing side of my battle against pornography. I felt hopeless at my worst moments, but confused at my best, because at those moments I was in sync with God and yet still having a hard time with this sin.

As a Christian I found that porn lost much of its power over me when I put it into its proper perspective. Porn is a distortion of sex. But the power I had given to porn in my life was distorted as well. I believed lies about pornography. I took porn and I put it on a pedestal, saying, "This is the one thing that can separate me from God." As a result, I was afraid of porn. It caused me undue anxiety. That anxiety gave porn power and made me feel more helpless. It also caused a stronger urge for coping mechanisms in me. Guess what the coping mechanism turned out to be most of the time? Porn.

Porn cannot separate you from the love of God. On this journey of freedom, you will most likely stumble once or twice. Refrain from getting mad or sad when you fail. Instead, pray and get up and keep moving forward. For the spouse of the addict during this healing process it can be very hurtful. Even though change is happening there are still sporadic failures in the early stages of the journey. The husband or wife of the addict needs to be prepared for a journey to healing and not a quick fix.

The other side to viewing porn as sin is saying that it's okay. While we don't use these words we are saying, "It's just the way God made me so keep it in moderation and don't worry." But as we've already seen, there is no moderation of pornography. A little porn is too much porn. The only way to ensure that no one watches porn is for each person to stop watching porn. You may not have control over other people, but you have control over yourself. You are the one participant in the victimization of those enslaved in the industry you can stop. You are the one who will be held accountable for your actions. You are the one who can choose to stop. Stop fantasizing about porn and be a real hero.

Chapter 9 Homework:

Answer the following question(s):

1. In what ways have you given porn more power in your life than it should have? How can you remove that inappropriate power in your life?

CLOSING THOUGHTS

We are all slaves to someone or something. If we try to be our own masters, then we are only the slaves to our own biochemistry. What is freedom in a world where everyone is a slave? Freedom is found in how much privilege our master gives us. All people are slaves, but not all masters are equal in their liberties and restrictions.

Pornography is a terrible master. It restricts our movements in the world. You want adventure: Can you live in the jungle without porn? It restricts our thinking: We are so consumed by it that it affects all other aspects of our lives and thoughts. It restricts our social interactions; we are ashamed and worried that people will find out about our secrets and we become apathetic about the pain of others. For some men and women it even keeps them jobless, spending hours on their computers.

As pornography viewers, we develop a relationship with porn, and we bond with our captor. We know it is bad for us, and yet we don't want to let it go–even to the point of defending it with excuses and lies.

A master, as strong as pornography, is not easy to kill. It will be a struggle. It will take time, but it is worth all the effort, and the fight is winnable. That's why prayer is so important because it will be a fight for some time. It is like a wounded animal who knows it is about to die, thrashing about to cause as much damage as it can. Fight against the easy path to "just forget about it." You can't forget about your manhood or womanhood and the duty to protect the vulnerable; your duty to not prey on them. You will hear a lie that says, "Not every girl or boy was from a broken family," but you can't forget that every girl or boy in porn is now trapped in brokenness. What is perhaps the most dangerous part of this process is the lie that says, "Just forget about the voice in your head." God will speak in your heart, not necessarily an audible voice from the natural world that moves your eardrum and then sends a signal to your brain; you will hear Him speak to you as if with an ear that hears only through understanding. This may not make sense to some readers, and that's fine–even if you don't believe in God just tune in to the truth and do not let yourself forget what you now understand.

After a short period of time, your mind will literally transform into something else. Once you kill off your desire to watch porn, you will be free and the lies will stop. The wonderful thing about this is that you are not killing your sexual desires, but you are killing your sinful nature. You are returning to the design that God intends. Pornography is an idol in the heart of everyone who watches it; it was in mine. Now my life is completely different.

I was not married when I first wrote this book. I still held to all the truths I presented and I still hold to them all these years later as a married man. The issue with singles is not sex but our perception of sex. Something happens to many young men that affects their view of sex. I can only speak for men here. Their parents are many times afraid to discuss real life issues with them and rarely get involved on this subject on a deep level. Young men hear about how sad their elder's lives are and how sex won't be a thing in their relationships when they get older. Young men become distraught because the teachings of the community they live in misrepresent what God gives us in sex. So, by default, they learn about their sexual identity from pop culture. They are exposed to things like pornography at a young age and are surrounded by sex from their peers. As a result, they become bitter at God and more terrified of Him. Because all they know is that they desire to have sex and yet they are told to simply turn it off by their family or conservative community. This worldview confusion causes a lot of unnecessary stress and further confusion in many young people. They are told to be less like themselves, but they are not told how to be more like Jesus. So how does an addict be more like Jesus and live as a single man or woman without watching porn?

The best action to take to become more like Jesus is to be a better servant as He was. You can sit down and think about how you will help the world, but just thinking won't change yourself or the world. Simply get up and start serving those around you, forgive those who wrong you even when it hurts for a time. Act love out in relationships and it will make a difference in your heart as you will become more selfless. But here's the thing: You have to act as a servant without expectations. Remember, porn is selfish. The fight against porn is a fight against selfishness.

So, I recommend that you get involved in your community and particularly with helping people who are hurting unless you have predatory feelings and in such a case you should not be helping them but seeking clinical and biblical help. Contact your local homeless shelter and make a meal or serve dinner and get connected in people's lives. This is especially important for men, as there is a dearth of good men who are virtuously ambitious in our society. Even if you don't feel a desire to go out in your community and get involved, do it regardless. You will find yourself motivated to go more once you start doing something. Our motivation to be a positive pillar in our community is like the Law of Inertia: An object at rest will stay at rest, until a force compels it to change. Once we start, we are motivated and will keep going. It's just the starting that can be difficult–that's why you simply have to do it.

Porn might make you sick now after you do it. But getting involved in the lives of others and taking a responsible role in your own life will cause porn to make you sick before you watch it. This is because it's not about the shame of being caught or guilt in the afterthought that makes you sick anymore. Now you are sick about the reality of how evil porn is and the damage it does on the people you are now loving and caring for. Your desire to participate will be gone.

Another important thing is to get involved with men or women who have overcome porn in the past. But get involved with people of your own gender. Go through this book and other good materials together but don't be alone. Follow the steps as a team and hold yourself accountable before each other and God. Don't lie to each other and don't use fake words to hide real meanings: If you watched porn, then you watched porn; if you masturbated, then you masturbated. Just be real about it and things will get better with time and a strong commitment to change will happen.

Ultimately, you will have to find a new master. This is where, whatever you believe, God is unavoidable.

Porn has been your master in this area of your life, maybe for a long time. As you kill it, then you will have to find a new master. Some men find a new master in work, and others in non-pornographic hobbies or in travel. But the truth is, while these things are good things, they, too, can become damaging like pornography to us and our families if they become our master. Jesus alone is the proper master for our lives.

When Jesus is first, everything else falls into place naturally. Things like not watching porn, which were once a burden, become natural when He is our master. I once thought that watching porn was an inescapable fate, something I was doomed to do for the rest of my life whether I wanted to or not. Now I am free from the desire to watch porn. I literally cannot believe who I was before.

The shift in my life has been from slavery to freedom. Like a slave who has recently been freed, I found myself with more time than I had before. It startled me. I had to readjust my thinking and time management. I realized how much time I'd spent watching and thinking about porn and instead I devoted that time to other pursuits. It is amazing how much you can learn by spending even a fraction of those hours watching porn and instead in reading books, learning languages, developing skills, praying, or just getting in the community. Ending a porn addiction will change your life.

If you allow Jesus to become your master and you take these steps to kill your desire for porn, then, in time, you will honestly not be able to recognize yourself or your life.

My final words to you are to pray for the hurting, act with honor, and never surrender.

www.ingramcontent.com/pod-product-compliance
Lightning Source LLC
Chambersburg PA
CBHW021148020426
42331CB00005B/949